WORDS OF
WISDOM

In Interest on Relationships

WORDS OF WISDOM

In Interest on Relationships

BISHOP JULIUS LA-ROSA GREEN

ARPress
ILLUMINATING IDEAS
EMPOWERING VOICES

ARPress
45 Dan Road Suite 5
Canton, MA 02021

Hotline: 1(888) 821-0229
Fax: 1(508) 545-7580

Ordering Information:
Quantity sales. Special discounts are available on quantity purchases by corporations,associations, and others. For details, contact the publisher at the address above.

Printed in the United States of America.

ISBN-13:   Softcover   979-8-89356-442-6
                      eBook   979-8-89356-441-9

Library of Congress Control Number: 2024904629

CONTENTS

Welcome

To an extraordinary and an incredible adventure of wisdom, knowledge, and understanding to help assist and encourage you to develop a well- balanced and long-lasting relationship or marriage. Also, to assist you, I have provided a variety of scriptures from the bible to read.

Remember

an achievable and flourishing relationship between partners, married or unmarried is put together and fastened by love. Wherefore, keep in mind that wheresoever love resides, God is present and because of God being in the midst and partners' compliance, He secures the alliance between them.

Love Bishop Julius La-Rosa Green

Dedication

This book is written in honor
of my wife Deborah Lynn Holloway Green

whom I truly and deeply miss. Nevertheless, I'll be alright
because I believe that she is in good hands and excellent care,
and that the Lord has sent at least two angels to safely escort
her into the rest that He has prepared and promised to those
that die in Him. _____

_____

_____

_____

_____

_____

_____

_____

_____

_____

_____

_____

_____ (Recommended reading: Hebrew 4:9-11.)

Love
Bishop Julius La-Rosa Green

Introduction

I've been inspired
and truly motivated by the Spirit

of the Lord to write this book. It has been designed to help strengthen and revitalize relationships amongst partners, and to provide some sort of therapy for shattered relationships or marriages around the world. Perhaps God for some time has been observing persons that are in relationships or marriages and recognized that they needed His help. Being inspired by the spirit of the Lord I constantly labored day and night; hour after hour convinced, that if the counseling in this book and its recommendations could reach persons, not only would it help assist in bringing about a positive change among partners, but also help to heal our nation. _____

_____

_____

_____

_____

_____

_____

_____

Love
Bishop Julius La-Rosa Green

Introduction

What's more,
the writing in this book is thoroughly

put together to make exceptionally clear to individuals that may be considering a relationship or contemplating on getting married about the task and responsibilities that are generally incorporated with being sincerely involved or connected to someone by marriage. Even so, whatsoever your intentions or the situation might be, there are so many unproductive and shattered relationships that contribute enormously to the ruins of so many marriages that are accountable for so many broken homes that are responsible for so many traumatized persons that are left imprisoned by the experience and impact of an unhealthy and devastating relationship. _____

_____

_____

_____

_____

_____

_____

Love
Bishop Julius La-Rosa Green

Introduction

Persons looking
for a partner should be cautious

whereas the hurtful experience some persons hold on to has the potential of bringing about dramatizing and problematic circumstances that not only have a devastating impact on their relationship or marriage but their lives as well. Spilling over and effecting our schools, neighborhoods, communities, churches, streets, cities, states, countries, etc. Nonetheless, I'm confident that the recommendations provided in this book will help to support persons that read and hold on to its knowledge and understanding with a durable and long-lasting relationship. Whereas dysfunctional partners married or unmarried in the end contribute to a dysfunctional society.

_____

_____

_____

_____

_____

_____

_____

Love
Bishop Julius La-Rosa Green

Introduction

Because of the
benefiting factors this book

brings to persons that are involved a relationship, married or
unmarried, I perceive the counseling provided regarding the
interaction between them will massively help to decrease the
expanding rate of traumatized marriages across the country,
which will as well assist in dropping the high percentage of
separation and divorce. Also, I'm optimistic by encouraging
better relationships it will as well decrease the growing rate of
poverty, cut down on the national and government's spending-
budget, prohibit the aggressive accelerating rate of violence
and teen pregnancy, and lower the expanding and high cost of
correctional institutions. _____

_____

_____

Words of Wisdom

How knowledgeable
were you regarding the rules, guidelines,
policies, and ethical principles of relationships when you first became involved with someone. Usually, persons involved in a relationship basically just make up the rules between them and the partner they are involved with as they go along. They as well anticipate that the involvement between them will last forever.

_____

_____

_____

_____

_____

_____

_____

_____

_____

Words of Wisdom

Partners that become
closely knitted, together in time
have children together, share their possessions, and welcome
their family, friends, and colleagues to become a part of their
social group. However, as you can see, regardless of all these
networking fulfillments between partners the preponderance
of innumerable relationships are still nonetheless short-term
involvements.

Words of Wisdom

Some partners
ponder the idea it's safer

to be somewhat affiliated with persons rather than to become morally joined to them. However, there are more difficulties, hardships, and unnecessary sufferings in relationships than marriage. Furthermore, despite the high-level rate of divorce, the ratio of fragmented relationships outweighs divorcement by a significant and incredible degree. You see, what marriage does is dissuades the hasty revolving door between partners. It as well serves as a covering that alleviates, safeguards, and secures the accomplishments shared by both partners. _____

Reflections

Words of Wisdom

Some persons
that are involved with one another

oftentimes, are reluctant to move ahead to marriage because they either were never actually honest about the relationship, or they conceivably were more committed to some preconceived and/or unprincipled belief of marriage. For this reason alone, a committed relationship among these types of partners, married, or unmarried are never truly established. _____

_____

_____

_____

_____

_____

_____

_____

_____

Words of Wisdom

In addition, partners
that are coupled with one another,

in this manner contribute substantially to the overwhelming and increasing rate of separation and divorcement. Therefore, it is not marriages that should be studied, but rather persons that are involved in a relationship and are not actually ready to commit.

Reflections

Words of Wisdom

The authentic purpose
of relationships in essence is designed
to eventually bring partners together who are prepared and
willing to dedicate and pledge themselves to one another by
marriage. However, as you can see, there are a great deal of
relationships, but very few and far between commitments. Even
as I am characterizing in writing concerning this problematic
and controversial catastrophe regarding partners, married, or
unmarried, some persons are either going into a relationship
or coming out of one. _____

_____

_____

_____

_____

_____

_____

Marriage is not
where the utmost configuring

and bringing together of persons who are involved with one another begins, but is instead, the relationship. You see the additives you both sow into your involvement together will automatically dictate the type of relationship you as partners, will jointly share together. The same is for marriage, it can only replicate that which both partners sows into the relationship. Wherefore, partners should be advised, sowing unhealthy additives, particularly of previous relationships has the tendency to intrude, undermine and dismantle the promising potentials of your existing relationship. _____

_____

_____

_____

_____

Words of Wisdom

As optimistic partners
that anticipate and are hopeful
of successfully achieving an uninterrupted relationship, you
should cooperatively spread nourishing ingredients into your
involvement with one another. In doing so, you both will be
able to reap the benefits from the harvest you mutually plant
and share together. _____

_____

_____

_____

_____

_____

_____

_____

_____

Reflections

Words of Wisdom

Finally, I would like to address
three most important key factors: 1) intimacy,

2) compassion, and 3) receptiveness. Predominantly, authentic intimacy extends beyond the bedroom and should not only be communicated in words, but in deeds as well. Intimacy is an exceptional ingredient that every person who is involved in a relationship desire. It is a feeling of being passionately and affectionately loved and appreciated. It as well has to do with partners being trustworthy of whom confidential matters are confided. _____

_____

_____

_____

_____

_____

_____

_____

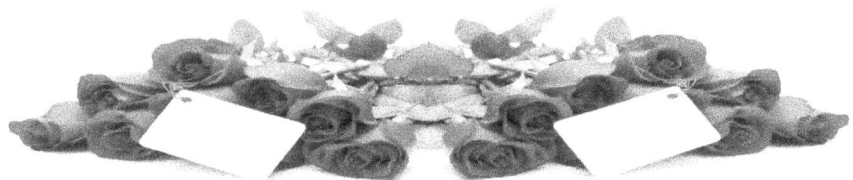

Words of Wisdom

The second key factor
is compassion. This is one of the
exceedingly favorable and refreshing factors of the relationship. The essential ingredients of this partner's factor have to do with the attendance and interaction of kindness, generosity, tenderness, warmth coziness, and affection between partners that motivates them to blend their hearts, minds, and souls together as one. It as well promotes the kind of unwavering closeness that steadfastly fastens them to God and with one another.

 *Words of Wisdom*

The third key factor
is receptiveness. This indispensable factor _____
has to do with partners being open-minded and responsive
to one another's ideas. However, if partners are not receptive
and thoughtful regarding one another's gestures, the fondness
that reinforces and safeguards the closeness between them
could conceivably go lacking until the exchange of thoughts
between them has been resolved. _____

_____

_____

_____

_____

_____

_____

Let's take

A glimpse at some additional words of wisdom in interest on

Relationships

Words of Wisdom

Persons
married, or unmarried,

should learn how to be reasonable and concerned about one another's feelings. In doing so this will enhance and invigorate their love connection with one another and motivate a fervent and an enthusiastic degree of love and appreciation towards God. Furthermore, should you as partners fasten yourselves to the idea of this factor and be steadfast, in time your affection towards one another will flourish and manifest an exceptional reflection of God's presence upon you both._____

_____

_____

_____

_____

_____

 *Words of Wisdom*

One of the most severe
and intense interruptions of relationships

is the inadequacy and absence of good communication. Good communication is crucially necessary to influence a healthy relationship between partners, married or unmarried. Good communication has to do with partners listening and hearing one another and responding to one another appropriately and respectfully. There are three things to keep in mind. To start with, as a couple you should never interrupt when the other is speaking, but rather be patient and let the other partner finish.

Words of Wisdom

You should
make sure to avoid belaboring
or going on and on with what you have to say, but rather give
the other partner a chance to respond. lastly, as partners you
should never be in pursuit of proving who's right or wrong,
but instead be honest, just, and fair, as you both together look
for answers and resolvents that will promote the balance of
your relationship.

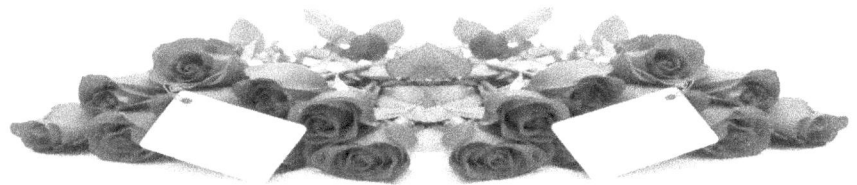

Reflections

Words of Wisdom

Partners listening
to one another is very essential.

However, partners really paying attention and hearing what one another is saying is of the utmost importance. Wherefore, it is seriously imperative that you as partners learn to do them both. Ultimately, when you as partners conduct yourselves in accord with that which is recommended in this segment, it will indicate that you as partners were not only listening, but you both also were paying attention and heard what one another had to say. In doing this it will assist you in finding ways to solve problems and move towards the next level of happiness.

 *Words of Wisdom*

As partners
you at times may experience,

altercations, in resolving difficulties, particularly when it comes to differences of opinions. If you both are not observant and cautious of such differences, it could cause you to plunge into emotional behaviors that in time will bring about unpleasant environments that will at intrude, interrupt, and diminish the harmony of your involvement, manipulating you both to feel uninterested in having anything to do with one another. ____

Words of Wisdom

When attempting
to resolve problems partners should _____

make sure to stick to the issue at hand and never ever bring up unresolved concerns to get their point across. Oftentimes the outcome of this course of action will only make matters much more complicated and the problem at hand more challenging and difficult to resolve. _____

_____

_____

_____

_____

_____

_____

_____

_____

Reflections

 *Words of Wisdom*

You've heard
of unconditional love, haven't you?

You see unconditional love is equivalent to the love that God provided and passed on to us through Jesus Christ. He despite our imperfections gave himself for our transgressions that we through him might have the opportunity to put an end to our flaws. Partners that share this inexplicable and unmeasurable love together should likewise disclose the same love towards one another. This form of love does not suggest that partners do not have to changed but rather gives partners that indeed care for one another an opportunity as well to put an end to their imperfections. _____

_____

_____

_____

 *Words of Wisdom*

The scriptural code
encrypted by God discloses unending knowledge

and recommendations that should be entirely embraced
and employed by both partners, married, or unmarried. By
them adopting and fully incorporating the authentic and true
meaning of unconditional love, they together will be able to
prevail over adversities that have impacted and contributed to
the failure of incalculable relationships, around the world. __

_____

_____

_____

_____

_____

_____

_____

Words of Wisdom

You're going to become
aware of one another's blemishes,

flaws, slipups, weaknesses, shortcomings, and imperfections, Nonetheless, by reverencing, and fulfilling God's example of unconditional love it will enhance, improve, and sustain the accountability of your relationship with one another. It alone will remarkably counsel you against cravings and imaginings of uncoupling passions and keep you from the pressures and attractions of immoral activities as well as persons that might take the involvement of their relationship for granted. _____

_____

_____

_____

_____

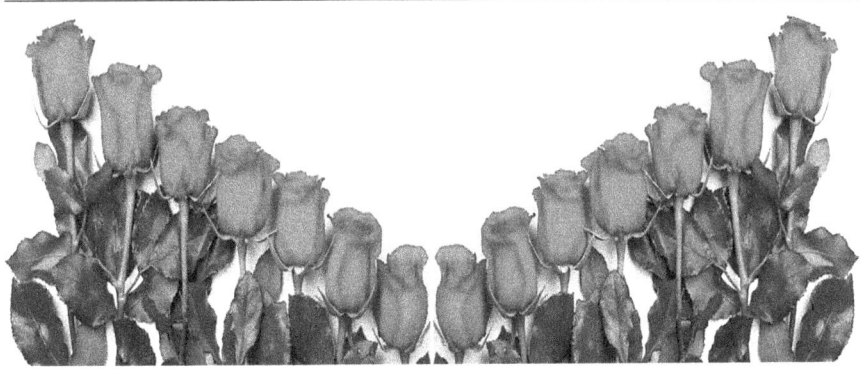

Reflections

Kind-hearted deeds
regarding unconditional love

gives you as partners the opportunity to make the necessary revisions in your relationship that bonds you closer together rather than distancing you. After all, just as marriage can be no greater or lesser than what God intended it to be, neither can relationships between partners married or unmarried be no more than the efforts they are both willing to put into it.

Words of Wisdom

That you as partners
may happily achieve your goal

of a successful relationship, you should operate in ways that compliment and authenticate your love for God and with one another. Despite appearing ill-advised to others, whereby, as being a team intertwined in Christ as a threefold cord, your relationship or marriage will remain sturdy, long-lasting and without interruption. _____

_____

_____

_____

_____

_____

_____

_____

 *Words of Wisdom*

For partners
to sincerely bond together as one, _____

they should learn to work together and adopt methods that provides for them as a team. They should keep in mind that they no longer function as a single entity but as an integrated enterprise, whereby, the success and longevity of their mutual involvement depends upon them both._____

_____

_____

_____

_____

_____

_____

_____

Reflections

Words of Wisdom

Intimacy
within relationships, married or unmarried,

is one of the riches, most prominent, and affectionate lifelines of your involvement. Partners that look for a promising and favorable relationship should never neglect or abandon such vital and indispensable closeness shared between them both.

Words of Wisdom

As partners,
you should become well-informed.

as well as prepared and willing to submit yourselves to the liabilities and obligations of relations before bonding together in marriage. Otherwise, the lack of knowing and unfulfilled marriage vows will in time, huff, puff, and blow your marital relationship down. _____

_____

_____

_____

_____

_____

_____

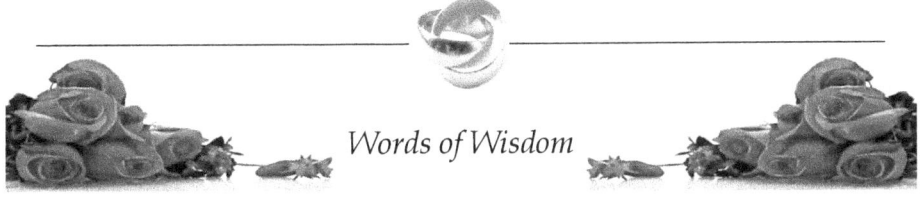

Persons involved
with one another including spouses
should abstain from day-and-night confrontations. For such relentless disputes causes tension and bring about conditions that has the potential to intrude upon, interfere with, and deter the productive teamwork between them, and sooner or later disassemble their relationship. _____

_____

_____

_____

_____

_____

_____

_____

_____

_____ (Rememended reading: 2nd Corinthians 13:11)

Reflections

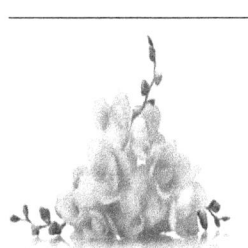

Words of Wisdom

Partners that notice
The intrusion of disturbances

inching in the middle of their alliance, married, or unmarried, should not be reluctant, postpone, or take such interruptions lightly, but rather work together to annul such disruption and restore the peace and harmony between them both. _____

_____

_____

_____

_____

_____

_____

_____

_____

_____

Words of Wisdom

Continuous confrontations
and unethical behaviors will gradually
eat away and devour the foundation of your relationship and eventually come to be overpowering and prevent any efforts to restore the union. Therefore, as partners you should never pressure or impose upon one another to endure irrational and unhealthy conditions, nor should you leave your partner no other alternative than separation and/or divorce. _____

_____

_____

_____

_____

_____

_____

 *Words of Wisdom*

It's not God's intent
that partners should suffer unfairly.

However, should you, as partners, married, or unmarried, be unwilling to communicate with God and with one another, in time you will leave yourselves with minimum or no room for reconciliation, and the probability of toning your relationship would be inconceivable because of zero cooperation. _____

_____

_____

_____

_____

_____

_____

_____

Reflections

Words of Wisdom

The perseverance
among partners including spouses

provides a greater and better reward than separation, and the preventable grief of divorce. Therefore, if you, that are joined together especially by God really love one another, you should seriously come together and resolve the problem, rather than separate and divorce. _____

_____

_____

_____

_____

_____

_____

Words of Wisdom

Practices that others
may have configured in relationship
might not necessarily be beneficial for you and your partner
and applying the same methods can at best lead you to the
same place. Therefore, as partners you should consider and be
willing to seek out fresh ideas and recommendations that may
work to help improve your relationship. _____

_____

_____

_____

_____

_____

_____

_____

_____

Words of Wisdom

Partners that pledge
themselves to God and one another, _____

should never ever expose themselves to others in ways that are improper, nor should you as partners conduct or express yourselves in manners that suggest you're not in a committed relationship, or that you are unmarried, but rather be completely faithful and honor your pledge to God and with one another. _____

_____

_____

_____

_____

_____

_____

_____

_____

Reflections

Words of Wisdom

As partners,
you should learn to submit

yourselves faithfully to God's reassured and durable ethics for partner's involvement and interactions. You should learn to embrace and become accustomed to its expertise. Incorporate its unique qualities, that will assist you as partners, married or unmarried, to increasingly merge and unify you together as one and prohibit the influences of immoral behaviors and activities upon your alliance together. _____

_____

_____

_____

_____

_____

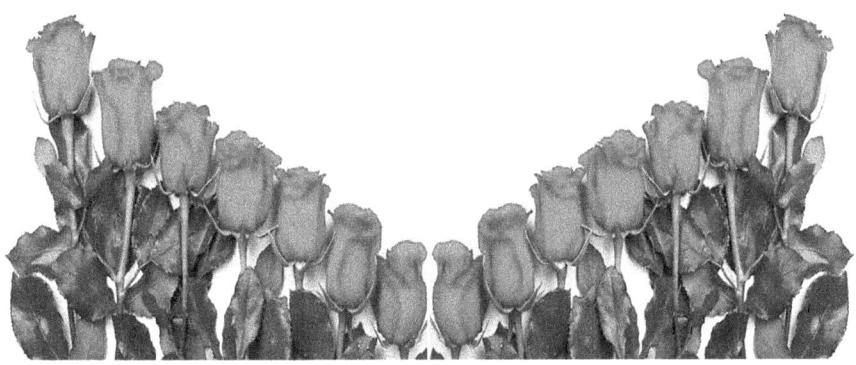

Words of Wisdom

Partners that meditate,
and are sincerely interest and endeavored

to practice the counseling and follow the guidelines of God's predetermined, and encrypted ethics for relationships under grace and truth shall have good success. _____

_____

_____

_____

_____

_____

_____

_____

_____

_____ (Recommended reading: Joshua 1:8)

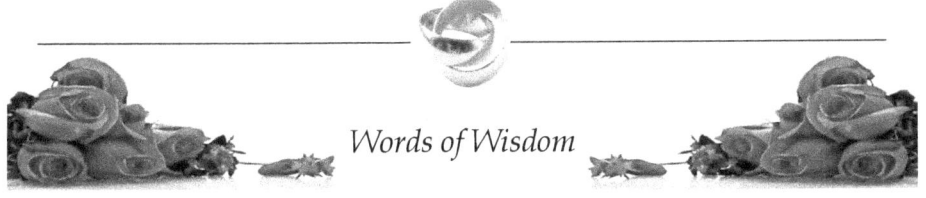

Words of Wisdom

Foolish and improper speaking
merely ushers' partners, married, or unmarried,

into unhealthy atmospheres of the adversary, who eventually drives them into aggressive environments that spontaneously feed off their feelings and emotions that are accompany with disorders that has the power to beguile and overthrow their interaction with one another. Therefore, as partners, married, or unmarried, you should be observant and cautious of how you converse with one another. _____

_____

_____

_____

_____

_____

_____

_____

Reflections

 *Words of Wisdom*

Thus, as Jesus Christ
has removed the influence of sin

from his body, so does he petition and expect you as partners that are connected to him and with one another, married, or unmarried to get rid of any form of immorality and deeds of infidelity from the moral ethics of your involvement together.

Words of Wisdom

"The eye of the Lord
is upon the righteous, and his ears

are open unto their prayers. The righteous cry, and the Lord
hears and delivers them out of all their troubles." So does the
Lord hear partners, married, or unmarried, who worship him
and do his will. Despite the difficult challenges partners may
face these days, the Lord will not abandon you. He will assist
you that are endeavored to abided by the counseling of his
recommendations to achieve a successful relationship. _____

_____

_____

_____

_____

_____

_____

_____ (Recommended reading: Psalm 34:15, 17, 19.)

Words of Wisdom

"Should partners
become beguiled by Satan's deception, _____

he could overcome them and drive their relationship out of the

presence and supervision of the Lord at any time. Therefore,

as partners you should be sober and vigilant, seeing that our

adversary the devil, walketh about, searching for unprotected

relationships he can wreck and destroy. _____

_____

_____

_____

_____

_____

_____

_____

_____

_____

_____ (Recommended reading: 1st Peter 5:8-9)

Reflections

Words of Wisdom

Partners, should reframe
from arguments and disappointing one another.

Whereas controversial conversations, bring about imbalances, and unfulfilled promises disappoint partners and dismantles their confidence. Thus, pertaining to these stumbling blocks, you as partners should remember that the longevity of your alliance does not require the determination of one partner, but the reliable and honorable efforts of both partners. _____

_____

_____

_____

_____

_____

_____

_____

Words of Wisdom

To effectively build
and maintain a good relationship
you should learn how to repent and be willing to forgive. In addition, you should be honest, just, and faithful, and not return to that which you asked to be forgiven of. Otherwise, such insulting, and rude behavior will generate grieved and hurtful feelings that will in the end undermine and ruin your involvement together. _____

_____

_____

_____

_____

_____

_____

 *Words of Wisdom*

Submission to God's counseling
and intervention for the good outcome
of reconciliation, requires the dutiful and endeavored efforts
of both partners. What's more, they should be observant and
watchful of areas from which division stems from, being that
separation and divorce is not a part of God's perfect will for
those he unites. _____

_____

_____

_____

_____

_____

_____

_____

_____

Reflections

Words of Wisdom

The unfluctuating unification
between partners, married, or unmarried,

has to do with their enthusiasm and willingness, as a couple,
to overcome harsh situations that invades and challenges the
resilience of their relationship and the durability and longevity
of their involvement together. _____

_____

_____

_____

_____

_____

_____

_____

_____

_____

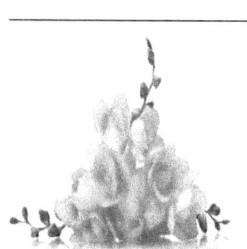

Words of Wisdom

Should partners sees
to cooperate with one another

according to God's recommended counseling for the success of a moral and prosperous relationship, they could erratically ruin their chances of preserving a nutritious alliance between them both. Therefore, partners should without skepticism have respect for God's intervention over them and their alliance __

Words of Wisdom

Married, or unmarried partners
should keep in mind that Christ, is head
of the man and is also head of the woman. If the man does not
truly submit to Christ being his head, then he cannot be trusted
or reliable to lead as God intended. Therefore, men and women
should keep in mind that their commitment to one another is
firstly established upon their individual accountability to God,
who is head over them both. _____

_____

_____

_____

_____

_____

_____

Reflections

Words of Wisdom

For partners
to successfully mature
and effectively better their relationship they should by means
of God's counseling for successful interactions cast aside their
philosophies and become acquainted with and acknowledge
God's recommendations for partners, married, or unmarried,
whereby, Christ have no effect upon partners or spouses that
assemble their relationship outside of his counseling. _____

_____

_____

_____

_____

_____

_____

_____

_____

_____

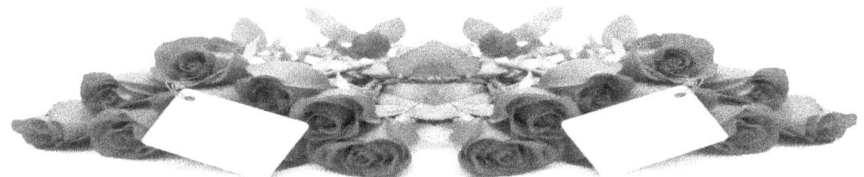

God knows
what's best for partners

that look forward to developing a long-term relationship and/
or a steady and solid foundation. As partners that anticipate
such end results, you should without question, or hesitation
comply with and follow God's recommendations, so that you
according to the advice of God's counseling might efficiently
accomplish what so many other promising partners, married,
or unmarried, have fallen short of. _____

_____

_____

_____

_____

_____

_____

Words of Wisdom

Persons in a relationship
should be careful of how they handle
_____
and care for one another, being that meeting a decent partner,

with a great personality, that honestly loves you, in these days

is most challenging and unbelievably difficult to identify. ___

_____

_____

_____

_____

_____

_____

_____

_____

_____

_____

Reflections

Words of Wisdom

The good seeds
are the children of the kingdom.

But the tares are the children that bear the distinct, nature, and behavior of the enemy. Therefore, when choosing a partner, to be affiliated with or joined to, be sure to remember the biblical description of both the physical and spiritual characteristics of the good seeds and the tares. _____

_____

_____

_____

_____

_____

_____ (Recommendation. Read: Mathew 13:37-39)

Words of Wisdom

Because of
the detrimental intent of the adversary

and his crusade to separate married, or unmarried, partners, particularly partners that dwell in the house of God. Persons involved with someone or even considering getting married, should first and foremost take a wide-range and an in-depth evaluation of the other partner's environments and associates before truly getting involved or saying I do. _____

_____

_____

_____

_____

_____

_____(Recommended reading: Judges 16:4-5, and 18-21.)

Words of Wisdom

Separation and divorce
is not God's idea or objective for partners.

However, in enormous circumstances, separation and divorce has been unavoidable because of the barbaric mistreatment of untold partners. Therefore, persons in relationship especially of the household of faith, should be endeavored to strive after God's recommendations for proper and healthy relationships and to prevent Satan's dethroning symptoms of separation and divorce.

Reflections

Words of Wisdom

God doesn't foresee
relationships as society views them.

Despite the impact of Satan's domestic attacks to degrade and undermine God's authentic and sacred grounds for partners, married, or unmarried. God's devout ruling for relationships, instituted under the moral principles and recommendations of grace and truth stands assured, and will never be destitute of its blessed and honorable significance. _____

_____

_____

_____

_____

_____

_____

_____

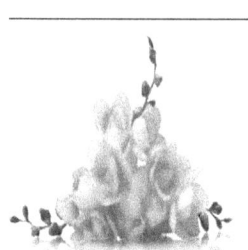

Words of Wisdom

So, partners may benefit
and be favored with uninterrupted interactions

with one another, they should decisively surrender and stick

to the vital principles and policies of God's recommendations

on the matter of obedience and the fulfillment of their role and

task within their alliance together. _____

_____

_____

_____

_____

_____

_____

_____

_____

_____

Words of Wisdom

The importance
of partners showing respect

to God's counseling regarding obedience indicate and reflect
his authority over your relationship as well as his supervision
over your involvement together. this assures you, as partners
that apply its sound values, and principles of an unbreakable
bond and a shatterproof alliance. _____

_____

_____

_____

_____

_____

_____

Reflections

Words of Wisdom

To disregard
or remove obedience from your alliance

would in time nullify God's way of balancing and effectively keeping you as partners attached. Thus, should complications descend upon your alliance, you would have no real solution to resolve the disabling effect nor overcoming the crippling impact, that have disassembled and caused the downfall of so many other relationships. _____

_____

_____

_____

_____

_____

_____

 *Words of Wisdom*

As partners,
you should incorporate

trust within your alliance so that you, as a team, may develop a loyal and devoted union that expresses an unquestionable unification and fellowship between God and you both. _____

_____

_____

_____

_____

_____

_____

_____

_____

_____

_____

God-fearing men should mainly be interested in women that acknowledges their role endorsed by God

(Recommended reading: Ephesians 5:22-24)

Men should be careful of taking notice of a woman's external features to determine her legitimate character.

They should as an alternative look upon that woman's heart whereas, her heart reveals a distinct assessment of who she really is.

(Recommended reading: Ephesians 5:22-24.)

Reflections

Men that expect
to receive God's approval and protection
that covers them and their families, should first surrender and give the highest recognition to Christ, who is their head and supreme mediator of their partner's association. _____

_____

_____

_____

_____

_____

_____

_____

_____

_____

_____

_____

Words of Wisdom

Respecting one another
is one of the most essential building blocks
of partner's relationships, that should never ever be disband
from their dealings with one another. Whereby, such neglect
of respect would in time open the doorway to impulsive and
unforgettable catastrophes. For that reason, partners should be
thoughtful of what they say, and how they express what they
want to convey. They should as well make sure to remove all
abusive exchanges of words from their conversations. In doing
so this will help you considerably with good communications
when dealing with discomforting and upsetting situations. __

 *Words of Wisdom*

To maintain
a healthy relationship

both partners should continue to walk in agreement with, and put into practice, God's advised recommendations, whereby, His therapeutic counseling for partners, married or unmarried will work out in your favor and for your good. In addition, by doing so, you will successfully achieve and preserve a durable and productive alliance together. _____

_____

_____

_____

_____

_____

_____

_____

Reflections

Persons involved
in a relationship, married, or unmarried,

should be observant of how they treat and consider each other's needs. Keeping in mind, that the same measures you expect and are hopeful to receive, should be the same measures you are willing to hold yourself accountable and answerable to.

_____

_____

_____

_____

_____

_____

_____

_____

Words of Wisdom

God fearing women
should bear in mind that Christ

is the supreme head. He is not merely head over the man but the woman also. Therefore, Women being precious, care for, and safeguarded by God's authority, should only surrender, and submit themselves to men that are respectful of and are obedient to God, who has placed them in the forefront, and expects them to lead in the manner that he commands them. Otherwise, women will be led into captive with no hope of a good relationship or salvation. _____

_____

_____

_____

_____

_____

_____

Words of Wisdom

Moral and honorable women
married or unmarried should be steadfast

and unwavering as regards to God's covenant blueprint for resilient and long-lasting connections between partners. You as well should be prepared and willing to comply with Your agreed responsibilities in the relationship. Whereby, through such compliance you may successfully achieve your goal of a fulfilling partners acquaintances by means of His grace, truth, and recommendations. _____

_____

_____

_____

_____

_____

_____

Reflections

Words of Wisdom

Women
that are hopeful of a successful relationship

should keep in mind that not every man honor or show respect to God's recommendations and essential counseling designed for the success of resilient relationships. For this cause, women should only make themselves and their aspirations noticeable and available to men that accept Christ as their superior head.

_____

_____

_____

_____

_____

_____

_____

_____

Words of Wisdom

Women that adopt
the characteristic of a meek spirit

and continue in its possibilities and soft touch shall not only bring about a sturdy balance to their relationship, but you in addition shall be extremely favored and blessed of the Lord. "Even as sara obeyed Abraham her partner, whose daughter ye are, so long as ye do well." _____

_____

_____

_____

_____

_____

_____

_____

_____

_____ (Recommended reading: 1st Peter3:6)

 *Words of Wisdom*

Partners should be
conscious of continuous conflicts.

They bring about discord that sooner or later get the better
of you, and pressure you as partners out of the company and
counselling of the Lord. Wherefore, you as partners, married,
or unmarried, should pursue tranquility, lets the beguilement
of the adversary through disputes overpower you and wreck
your relationship. _____

_____

_____

_____

_____

_____

_____ (Recommended reading: 1st Peter 3:11.)

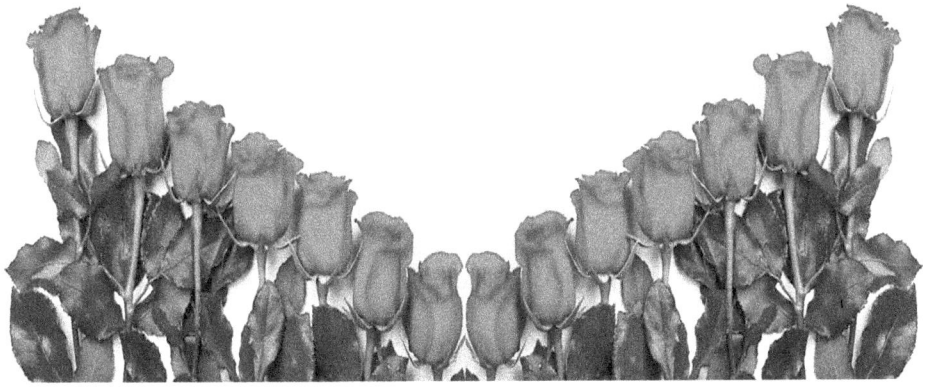

Reflections

Words of Wisdom

Looking after your needs while the desires and needs of the person you are in relations with, are overlooked is inappropriate and all wrong.

Besides, this disrespect in the end will merely convince and cause your partner to see you as selfish and unfair.

Therefore, remember to love your partner as you would want to be loved by God and cared for by them.

 *Words of Wisdom*

The impact
and effect of dramatic syndromes

can be associated with and infused by menopause which is a chemical imbalance. These intense and dramatizing emotions can have a shocking and devastating effect on the outcome of relationships. Wherefore partners especially marital partners should be observant and acquire the information about these emotional disorders lets the adversary uses these conditions to get the best of your alliance and devour your relationship. __

Words of Wisdom

Partners
Should consider God's recommendations.

However, should partners, married, or unmarried, prefer not to go along with God's recommendations and counselling for successful relationships. The consequences, and outcome of their alliance at that point, based on their decision, is in their own hands. Thus, breaching the covenant contract between them and God, compromising their intended position as God planned, and annulling any conceivable promises set in place by God for their good success. _____

_____

_____

_____

_____

_____ (Recommended reading: Mathew 12:25.)

Reflections

Words of Wisdom

Women that encounter
honorable and God-fearing men

that are interested in spousal relations, should make certain
they themselves also are interested, virtuous, well- informed,
and intellectually equipped with God's recommendations for
successful alliances. In that way you both may be compatible
partners that can attain a productive and prosperous marriage.

_____

_____

_____

_____

_____

_____

_____

_____

_____ (Recommended reading: Proverbs 11:16.)

Words of Wisdom

Moral and honorable
men should never give into indecency

If so, who would be around to encourage other men. their sons, and their son sons. Despite their shortcomings, they nonetheless can prevail. Listen even thou you may have fallen, it doesn't mean it should be the final story of your life, but you can rise upon your feet, and be endeavored to succeed, so that you can have the last say so, and a better ending to the final chapter of your life. _____

_____

_____

_____

_____

_____(Recommended reading: Psalms 37:23-24.)

Words of Wisdom

Some persons may say
"You can look, but don't touch."

But I say when your mind has been captivated by looking, and your feelings has been aroused with immoral thoughts, and imaginations, you have already touched or been touched. Therefore, partners should be cautious of how they observe others, for such inappropriate looking bring about tempting desires that leads to quarrels and split-ups between partners.

_____

_____

_____

_____

_____

_____

_____(Recommended reading: Mathew 5:27-28.)

Reflections

Words of Wisdom

Should it be your aim
to protect and preserve the allegiance
of your alliance from being lured into provocative and toxic
environments, you should without hesitation work together
to barricade one of the topmost venomousness and beguiling
snares pertaining to partners, married or unmarried. "Lustful
desires." _____

_____

_____

_____

_____

_____

_____

_____

_____

_____ (Recommended reading: Romans 13:13-14.)

Words of Wisdom

Persons
involved in a relationship
with Christ and with one another should learn self-discipline by focusing upon their way of thinking. You should as well be observant about looking upon others in an inappropriate manner which stir-up lustful desires, that are not in the best interest or favor of the partner you are presently with. _____

_____

_____

_____

_____

_____

_____

_____

_____ (Recommended reading: James 4:7.)

 *Words of Wisdom*

We live in a society
that encourages immorality.

Some persons say, "Practice safe sex" but I say, "Practice safe thoughts" whereby, if you can change the way you think, you can change the way you behave; if you can change the way you behave, then you can change the overall outcome of your life and relationship with Christ and with one another. Keep in mind, clear thinking is safe thinking. _____

_____

_____

_____

_____

_____ (Recommended reading: Proverbs 23:7.)

Reflections

Words of Wisdom

Your word is your bond.
therefore, you should say what you mean
and mean what you say. Yet should there arise instances that
inhibit you from honoring your promise, you should without
dragging your feet, communicate with the person in whom
you gave your word, to reassure them of your true intentions
of keeping and fulfilling your promise. _____

_____

_____

_____

_____

_____

_____

_____

_____

_____

_____ (Recommended reading. Mathew 5:37.)

Words of Wisdom

To disregard
the implementation of this factor
_____

that helps to enhance the character and bond between you as partners, would, sooner or later, breach the harmony of your interconnection with one another and in the end get the best of your alliance. Therefore, be sure to fulfill your promise to one another, less such broken promises huff, puff, and ruin your relationship. _____

_____

_____

_____

_____

_____

_____

_____

_____ (Recommended reading: Proverbs 31:10-11.)

Words of Wisdom

Trust is one of the most
important and essential factors
_____
within relationships. Moreover, trust determines whether the
involvement of your relationship will be long-lasting or short
term. Therefore, as partners, you should uphold and abide by
the qualities of trust whereby, your confidence in, and loyalty
to one another is unshackled and made free from all doubt. __

_____

_____

_____

_____

_____

_____

_____

_____

_____ (Recommended reading: Proverbs 3:5-6.)

Reflections

Words of Wisdom

Partners that consider
and implement God's advice on trust

should without uncertainty, honestly come together so that
Christ, as your mediator and advocator, may fully fasten you
with one another and reassure you as partners of a long-term
relationship, that is purged from the activity of cheating and
dishonoring one another. _____

_____

_____

_____

_____

_____

_____

_____

Words of Wisdom

Self-conceited,
self-loving, Self-caring, and self-serving
are all divisive and ill-mannered behaviors that give birth to catastrophes and breakdowns in relations especially marital relationships. Therefore, you that are combined as a couple should keep in mind that you are no longer single but are rather connected to someone other than yourself, and that part of your interaction with one another as partners is to learn how to share and to consider each other. _____

_____

_____

_____

_____

_____

_____

_____

Words of Wisdom

Should partners
pierce holes in their relationship
it would be equivalent unto a ship that couldn't prevent its passengers from drowning because of the holes they inflicted into the ship. Therefore, comparison to the ship, partners who inflict holes into their relationship they as well will sooner or later be submerged into floods of catastrophes whereby such calamities will drown any chances or efforts for an achievable relationship. _____

_____

_____

_____

_____

_____

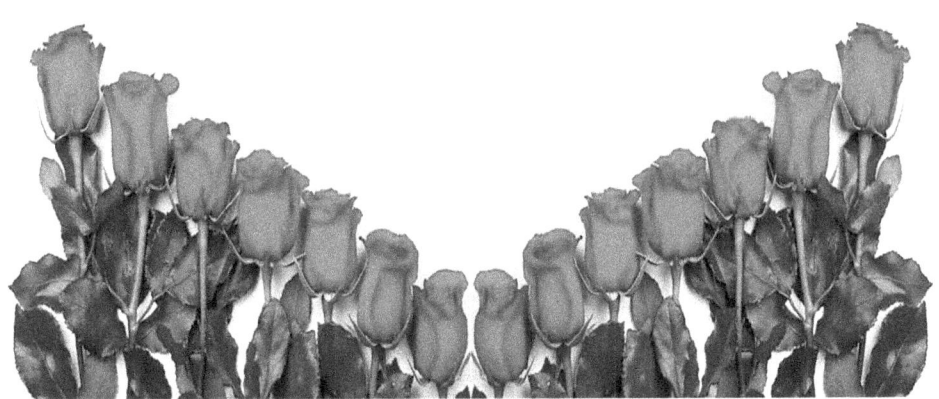

Reflections

Words of Wisdom

Rather than
puncturing holes into your relationship, _____

you should instead come together and reason. As partners You should learn to live peacefully with one another, sharing your time, feelings, and goals. You should bear in mind that you have been privileged to share God's grace on earth and that he requires and expects you to abstain from behaviors that lead to separation and/or divorce. _____

_____

_____

_____

_____

_____

_____

_____

_____

_____

_____ (Recommended reading: Colossians 3:15.)

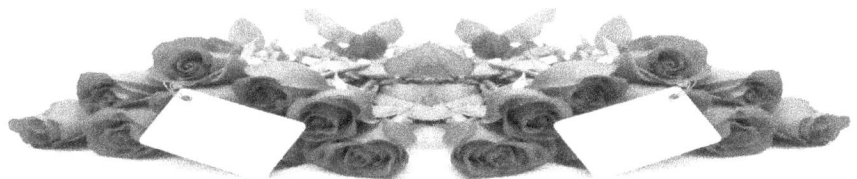

 *Words of Wisdom*

Maybe you've become comfortable with involving rude

and discourteous speeches in your discussion that you now depend upon them to assist you in expressing your feelings and to give you the advantage in confrontations. Nonetheless, speaking in such disrespectful manner to resolve problems only make matters worse. Therefore, as partners you should rehearsal and practice good communication, so that you may get away from offensive discussions that merely bring about detrimental outcomes. _____

_____

_____

_____

_____

_____

_____ (Recommended reading: Ephesians 4:31-32.)

Words of Wisdom

Dealing with
controversial altercations as partners

you should learn how to settle down so that you want speak or act in ways that you will later on regret. You should keep in mind how you both considerably love one another. and that the resilience of your love for one another is greater than the confrontation. This will provide you both with healthier thinking to cope with the confusion you face. Not as enemies but rather as a corporate team, working in harmony to prevent the aggressiveness of the enemy from bringing you both into his atmosphere. _____

_____

_____

_____

_____

_____ (Recommended reading: Mathew 18:19-20.)

Reflections

Words of Wisdom

Pointing out
the other partner's blemishes

and disregarding One's own flaws is all wrong. Furthermore, moving on to the next relationship without honestly assessing and adjusting your own imperfections will simply lead you to the same place, which is separation and/or divorce. _____

_____

_____

_____

_____

_____

_____

_____ (Recommended reading: Mathew 7:3-5.)

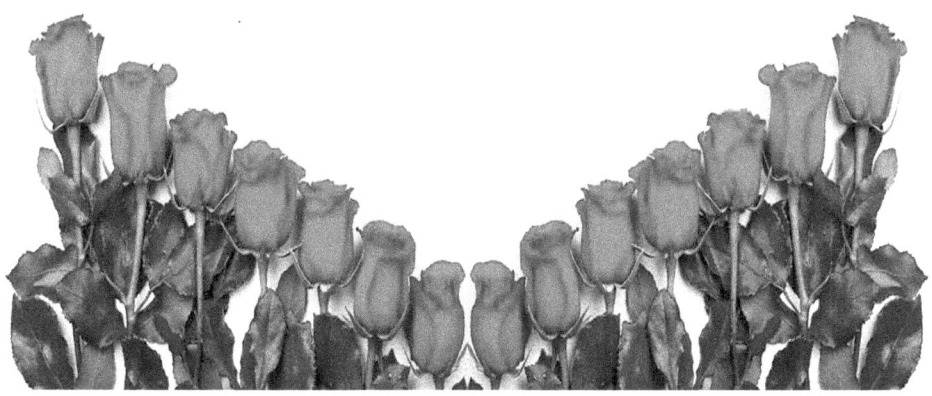

Words of Wisdom

Episodes
of previous unfavorable relationships
conceivably may have driven you to striking out at others in unseemly ways. Even so, it is still in your favor and best interest to accept, adopt, and incorporate God's recommendations that are essential for a healthy and successful covenant relationship with God and among one another. _____

_____

_____

_____

_____

_____

_____

_____ (Recommended reading: 1 Thessalonians 5:21.)

 *Words of Wisdom*

There are all sorts
of arrangements made available
for partners, married, or unmarried nowadays. Nonetheless, God's protocol and preordain recommendations, under grace and truth, exceeds them all. They in addition reassures partners that stick to its advice, of a long-lasting relationship without a termination date. Therefore, partners remember, to reflect on, adopt, and include the wisdom of this advice also. "Healthy communication stems from good conversations." _____

_____

_____

_____

_____ (Recommended reading: Isaiah 1:18-19.)

Reflections

Words of Wisdom

Getting involved
with someone devoid of an agreement
of a relationship is equivalent to an egg without the yolk. Just
as the egg yolk within the shell characterizes the true existence
of the egg, truly being an egg, so does the relationship among
partners serve as the most significant source that characterizes
and validates a true existence of their involvement together.
Therefore, without the proof of both, the connection between
partners is unfulfilling, and the egg or marriage is only a shell.

Words of Wisdom

Unthinkable challenges
and problems that partners, married or unmarried
face in society today, do not require one partner's attention,
but both partner's care. If they together can change the way
they think, they can change the way they behave too. If they
can change the way they behave, then, they as an alliance can
change the total outcome of their involvement together and
secure their relationship. _____

_____

_____

_____

_____

_____

_____

Words of Wisdom

Partners should keep
a personal diary of memorable moments

so that whenever they reflect on the events, they both shared together, the unforgettable remembrance of such events will overflow their hearts with so much happiness and overjoyed laughter, and right then you'll began to realize and appreciate the partner you desired to spend your life with was the right one.

124

Reflections

A relationship is like black-eyed peas and cornbread, peanut butter and jelly, salt, and pepper, ice cream and cake.

these ingredients are mixed together to bring out the most excellent and distinctive additives of one another.

Thus, like these ingredients so should partners be joined together, so that they as well, might bring out the finest and best traits in one another and live happily ever after.

Relations amongst partners devoid of a commitment is
parallel to one "who built his house upon the sand."

"And the rain descended, and the floods came, and the
winds blew, and beat upon that house.

and great was the fall of it, "for house was built upon
the sand. (Recommended reding: Matthew 7:26-27.)

Some persons suppose
that love is blind, but I say love has exceptional sight.
Some suggest that love is weak, but I decree that God is
love and that his indestructible love is superior, and his
strengths are without measure

Moreover, God's thoughts
and exceptional eyesight is without flaw.
Whereby, he foresees and prophesies, the past, present,
future, and even unpredictable intentions and feelings
of others.

Therefore, before agreeing
to a relationship or a marital partner,
you should study, and trust in the counseling of God's
recommendations, that you may choose wisely.

Reflections

Words of Wisdom

Study the advice
of these recommendations

until you have successfully contained and incorporated
the wisdom, knowledge, and insight of its moral values
and principles.

Whereby,
should you be in pursuit of a partner

or spouse, you may encounter someone that as well has
interest in a partner, based on God's recommendations

that will esteem, respect, and love you as God intended.

(Recommended reading: John 13:34-35.)

Reflections

Reflections

Reflections

Reflections

Reflections

Reflections

Reflections

Reflections

Reflections

Reflections

Words of Wisdom

Certificate
of Achievement

This certificate is presented to

_____

who has completed this book and retained

its wisdom.

May the Lord bless

and keep you.

*from:*_____

date:__ / __ / __

Forthcoming projects

Look for my new song on the CD The Lord's Way. This heart- fulfilling song is intended to reach out and touch the hearts of others who may not have been reached by other artists. What's more, this song is comforting and uplifting. Regardless of what you've been through, I'm sure that God will encourage you through this song so that you may change the outcome of your life through him. To get your copy, go to www.cdbaby.com.

Look for my new book, *Divorce vs. Covenant Marriage*. It's motivational, uplifting, funny, and overflowing with wisdom. It's a great tool, particularly for pastors who do counseling on challenging marital problems. Everyone should have a copy of this book in their homes and reading collection. If you don't have one, you should get one; you won't regret it.

Visit us at bcogfamilyoutreach.blog.com and take a look at our "Love is not something you can buy, but rather something you should give" fundraiser T-shirts.

To get your T-shirt, make donations payable to

The Bibleway Church of God Family Outreach
2733 Tidewater Drive
Norfolk, VA 23509

You can also donate at bcogfamilyoutreach.blog.com or call 757-718-7324.

Remember, "Addressing the complexities we now face in society does not require one person's attention, but everyone's care."

Thank you for your interest and support.

Bishop Julius L. Green